Storefronts & Facades

Martin M. Pegler

No. 7

Visual Reference Publications, Inc. ▪ New York

Visual Reference Publications
302 Fifth Avenue
New York, NY 10001

Distributors to the trade in the United States and Canada
Watson-Guptill Publishers
1515 Broadway
New York, NY 10036

Distributors outside the United Sates and Canada
HarperCollins International
10 E. 53rd Street
New York, NY 10022

Library of Congress Cataloging in Publication Data:
Gourmet & Specialty Shops
Printed in Hong Kong
ISBN 1–58471–053–5
Designed by Dutton & Sherman

Contents

Introduction

Architecture has always fascinated me. While others may wander through forests and glens breathing in deeply the miracles of nature, I am usually happier inhaling the fumes of taxis and trucks while walking on concrete pavement on streets in towns and cities. I am absorbed by and overwhelmed by architecture; by the buildings, structures and other man-made caprices that have lasted through many decades and, sometimes, even centuries. When I was a student—many, many, years ago—I majored in Interior Design , but the college I attended was a school of architecture so, like it or not, we were given a most catholic background in the History of Architecture. What I was taught stuck and affected me more than I imagined; thus, my deep respect and admiration for that art form and its practitioners.

For this, the seventh edition of Storefronts and Facades we have reverted to the format used in Volume Four. Taking quotes from my very first book, originally published in 1966 and revised in 1985, "Dictionary of Interior Design," we have taken classic and contemporary styles, designs, motifs, building materials and techniques and shown how they have been sources for new creations. Using the same motif or material, we offer "variations on a theme." We have shown how working in different areas, different countries, with different clients under assorted and diverse situations, architects and designers come up with distinctive and effective design solutions that are unique even though they all started out from the same, basic inspiration. Sometimes it is the material, the surfacing finish or even the color that makes the differences and sometimes it is the addition of light, the sizzle of neon, bright metallic trim, awnings or canopies that distinguishes the facade or storefront.

This book is really a collection of options; of ways to go or directions to take when designing a storefront or facade that has to make a definitive "opening statement." That is what Storefronts and Facades are all about—OPENING STATEMENTS. For the first edition of this series I wrote the following and I think it best sums up why this book has been assembled.

"Think of a storefront or facade as an overture to a musical comedy. It is the first impression you get of the sound, melodies and sights you are about to enjoy. It is a collage—a snipping together of various elements: graphics, building concepts, textures, lights and accents to create what is the essence of what is beyond the opening. The materials that are used and how they are used—the color inherent in those materials or applied to them or used with them to embellish the design—the graphics, the signage, the fenestration, the awnings and the plantings—they are all part of what the store is— what kind of services are available inside—the food or merchandise available beyond the portals. It is the IMAGE of that enclosed space that steps forward to meet the consumer on the street,in the mall or out on the highway."

We hope you enjoy this new edition; it has been a long time since the previous one was published. Use what you can of these concepts but give what you use your own personal artistic and creative interpretation and who knows—your NEW designs may be in Volume 8 of Storefronts & Facades.

Martin M. Pegler, SVM

Storefronts & Facades

Arches

A

B

The arch may be classically Roman in the History of Architecture but it still represents a graceful and elegant opening in walls of masonry. Rodeo Drive, in Beverly Hills, is noted as an enclave of upscale retail shops while the Bellagio Hotel and Casino in Las Vegas is as refined as it gets in Las Vegas. The Rodeo Drive streetscape, designed by The Jerde Partnership, reflects the look of an 18th century street brought into the vernacular of today while the designers of the Bellagio have created the feeling of an Italian Renaissance village as we might imagine it to look. The arched openings, in both constructions, salute the past as they add the elegant and graceful lines that please the eye and raises the spirit.

A/B/C:	RODEO DRIVE, *Beverly Hills, Los Angeles CA*
D/E:	BELLAGIO HOTEL & RESORT, *Las Vegas, NV*

D

E

C

Alexander, a chain of upscale fashion shops for affluent German women, uses the molding trimmed arch as its signature facade statement wherever the store may be located. When the arch adapts easily to the architecture of the existing building it can become an arcade of display windows as it is in the Munich store. In Heidelberg, the multi-storied shop relies on the arch to serve as a sweeping frame over the mall facing display windows on the upper level.

A big sweep of a Romanesque arch creates either a dramatic entrance statement as it does for the Nike store on E. 57th St. in New York City or it can humanize the bulk of the "big box" construction that is Byerly's upscale market. In both instances the arches are framed by brick masonry.

The late 19th century architecture of Amsterdam's Main Post Office now is the home to a downtown mall. The high flying arches, on the interior, are used to highlight such high-tech, youth oriented shops like America Today—pictured here.

A:	ALEXANDER • *Munich, Germany*
B:	BYERLY'S • *Maple Grove, MN*
C:	ALEXANDER • *Heidelberg, Germany*
D:	NIKE • *E. 57th St., New York, NY*
E:	AMERICA TODAY • *Amsterdam, The Netherlands*

A

B

C

D

E

A

"Downtowns" all along the eastern seaboard—and in other urban centers of the U.S.—are once again being revived and restored as Cultural and shopping centers. City Councils, Art Councils and Landmark Commissions are joining forces to save the handsome old buildings that add not add history to the streetscape but variety to the street architecture. Binghamton, NY—in upper New York State is one such city and shown here are the arch enriched, Romanesque-inspired, brick buildings with Victorian influences that were built at the end of the 19th century-early 20th century. Recently revived and refreshed, pointed and painted, they are ready to be inhabited and to be admired. Note how some of the undistinguished, mid 20th century buildings that stand amongst the Grandes Dames have been given new facade interest with arches floating over the brickwork. Now they complement the ancient structures.

On West Broadway, in New York City, landmark cast iron buildings of the 19th century stand shoulder to shoulder with "faceless" upstarts of the 20th century. Picking up on the combination of brickwork and Romanesque style arches, the new designer shops have updated their facades so that contemporary as they may be, they still sit comfortable and companionably with the period matrons.

A/B/C/D: DOWNTOWN • *Binghamton, NY*

E/F: WEST BROADWAY • *New York, NY*

B

C

D

E

F

A

The lighter side of the weight bearing arch: Shown here are examples of the arch used to affect a fun and playful feeling. Whether it is the red accented arches of an old B&B in a small town in Arizona or a series of in-your-face arches facing Melrose Ave. in Los Angeles, the result is the same.

On Main St. in Venice, CA the tired old buildings that have stood for decades are brightened up with rhythmic arcades of arches parading across the renovated facades.

At All American Sports, the NASCAR Speedpark boasts of corrugated aluminum lined arches that create tunnel-like entrances to a fun experience.

Classic Rome was never quite like the Grand Victorian Casino where the classic elements are exaggerated and overstated and presented in technicolor for fun seekers.

B

A:	MELROSE AVE • *Los Angeles, CA*
B:	RED GARTER B&B • *Williams, AZ*
C:	GRAND VICTORIAN
D:	MAIN STREET • *Venice, CA*
E:	ALL AMERICAN SPORTS • *Las Vegas, NV*

C

D

"arch: a curved or arced structural device spanning an opening. The arc may span the space between two walls, columns or piers and provide an opening such as a window or entranceway."

E

Art Deco

A

Art Deco has been described as "cubism—an early 20th century art movement—tamed and refined." Cubism gave it its shape and the Russian Ballet gave it its color. There were influences from the exotic: from the Egyptians, from the Congo and from the Mayans. Art Deco is an eclectic style that borrowed from many cultures, many countries and many design expressions.

South Miami Beach is a particular expression of the Art Deco style that blossomed there in the 1920s and 1930s. Shown here are some of the curves, sweeps, repetitive bands and motifs, floral inspired bas-reliefs, the cubism and "tamed exoticism" that has become the look of an era and of this special area. Mostly white with splashes of brilliant accents of turquoise, sunny yellow, salmon-pink and green, these "jewels" still stand and some have been rehabbed into retail outlets for designers and brand names while others serve as hotels and office suites.

A–F: SOUTH MIAMI BEACH • *FL*

B

C

D

E

F

Art Moderne

The art and style of the 1940s is when Art Deco gave way—somewhat—to the streamlining influences of modern travel. The sleek movement of autos racing along the road or airplanes swooping through space was captured in the lines of the buildings of this period. This period had its greatest impact on movie facade design and on the diners that became part of the highway scenery. Here are some original, old designs and some newly created art moderne tributes.

The Star Theater, designed by David Rockwell captures the colors, the sweeps and swells and the repetitive motifs that made Art Moderne so popular. Compare this to the stylized new Cinema in Kentland Shopping Center or to the refreshed Cameo movie house on Washington Ave. in South Miami Beach with its glass block front.

The Argentine Grill on Melrose Ave. and the music store in Westwood Village pay tribute to the early, diner-style architecture.

The streetscape of the old Hollywood in the MGM sector of Disney World stylishly recreates the period when movies were bigger than life and life attempted to be the movies.

C

B

A

A:	STAR THEATER
B:	CINEMA • *Kentland S/C, MD*
C:	CAMEO THEATER • *Washington Ave., So. Miami Beach, FL*
D:	ARGENTINE GRILL • *Melrose Ave., Loa Angeles, CA*
E:	MUSIC STORE • *Westwood Village, Los Angeles, CA*
F:	MGM • *Disney World, Orlando, FL*

F

E

D

Art Nouveau

The "new art" that took hold of Europe—especially in Brussels, Paris and Vienna—in the 1890s was dubbed Art Nouveau. It was a style of architecture and decoration based on flat patterns of twisting, tortured plant forms based on a naturalistic concept. Among the prime forces in the movement were Horta, Van de Velde, Charles Rennie Macintosh, Hector Guimard and Antonio Gaudi.

Illustrated here are some of the Art Nouveau treasures still standing and functioning in Brussels. Note the art-work, the metal grillwork and the whiplash motif that almost defines the period. Today we find elements of Art Nouveau design in shop fronts and facades where the architect/designer wishes to make a direct appeal to an upscale, elegant and sophisticated female clientele.

A

B

C

A–F: BRUSSELS • *Belgium*

E

F

D

Awnings

A

Awnings are bright, colorful "flags" that project out and over shop fronts and entrances to add color, pattern and even the shop's name to the public. By color or design the awning can be a shopper-stopper as evidenced in Friday's in Lima, Peru where the exciting architect/designer Orrega Herrera uses the red and white boldly striped, rigidly framed awnings to create an architectural statement in an otherwise, cube-like building. The panels of blue make a striking contrast to the red and white while affecting a kind of U.S.A. bravado that appeals to the younger patrons. The awning stripes are repeated with as much vigor on the giant sun-brellas over the patio dining tables.

A.G. Ferrari takes a strong step forward with the rich sienna-orange awning that not only plays up the store's signature color but the logo as well, which is imprinted on the awning. The floral display, outside, is not an afterthought but part of the design scheme.

Nacho Mamma's workmanlike and uninspired brick facade disappears while the eye-popping, strident, clashing and attention demanding colors of the pop-art inspired awnings step forward. The work of Sayles Graphic Design, the same vivid colors are introduced on the woodwork and doors to the café.

Another early 20th century building, this one in the Chelsea section of New York City, becomes a noticeable attraction thanks to the blue and green awnings with white ducks waddling across them. The crisp white painted window and door frames to Trois Canards picks up on the ducks that make more appearances on the canvas painted panels patterned over the red brick building.

A/B:	FRIDAY'S • *Lima, Peru*
C:	TROIS CANARD • *8th Avr., Chelsea, New York, NY* DESIGN • *Ohashi Design Studio*
D:	A.G. FERRARI • *San Francisco, CA*
E:	NACO MAMMA DESIGN • *Sayles Graphic Design*

B

C

D

E

A

Awnings can add a touch of class to a building and help define the tenant. The plastic panels extending out from over the British Museum Shop's display windows add a smart, contemporary look to the classic building's details which are now camouflaged by the black enamel paint. The plastic awnings serve as rain shields and also cut down on the glare while providing a clean, sleek look.

The elongated sweeps of white canvas over the windows of Comfort imply a stylishness and upscale quality to the casual dining experience. The very tall windows afford the designer the opportunity of using these angled exclamation marks on the facade.

The classic Willard Hotel in Washington, D C provides an adjacent home for the Chanel boutique. The crisp white awnings with the Chanel name or the logo in black are discreet while still making emphatic statements about who is in residence here.

In the elegant shopping experience that is the Bellagio retail area, La Perla uses cornice-like awnings, upholstered and braid trimmed, to create an intimate, boudoir-like setting for its elegant lingerie and nightwear. The cornices step forward over the building line without offense but with subtle color and restrained design.

B

A: CHANEL • *Willard Hotel, Washington, DC*

B: COMFORTS • *San Anselmo, CA*
         DESIGN • *Ohashi Design Studio*

C: BRITISH MUSEUM SHOP • *London, UK*
         DESIGN • *Carte Blanche*

D: LA PERLA • *Bellagio, Las Vegas, NV*

D

Bas Relief

A

Bas Relief is a form of sculpture in which designs are raised up from the background. It was a technique much used in classic architecture and has reappeared in other periods and decorative styles. Shown here are some examples where the bas relief was used to ornament buildings built in the 20th century.

Bas relief panels were used decoratively in art deco buildings and several examples are shown from South Miami Beach and from Los Angeles in CA. In Disney's MGM area the recreated streetscape also features some of the same treatment as is still evident in the El Capitan Theater on Hollywood Blvd. in Los Angeles.

A/B:	WOLFSON MUSEUM • *Washington Ave , South Miami Beach, FL*
C:	MELROSE AVE • *Los Angeles, CA*
D:	EL CAPITAN THEATER • *Hollywood Blvd., Los Angeles, CA*
E/F:	MGM STREET • *Disney World, Orlando, FL*

B

C

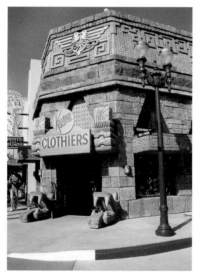

E

F

D

Bows & Bends

A soft turn in the masonry or glass—a sweeping expanse of facade breaking away from anchoring vertical blocks—these are the bows and bends that make contemporary architecture not only warm and human-scale but adds a gracious ambiance to malls and shopping centers.

Kaliedescope, a modern open shopping center designed by Altoon + Porter Architects is filled with soft curves, unexpected swings and dramatic circular focal points.

ELS/Elbasani & Logan Architects created this exciting, invigorating and yet inviting Crate & Barrel store in the Stanford Shopping Center. Angles and curves are combined with a striking glazed area to affect a memorable building.

A/B/C: KALEIDESCOPE • *Mission Viejo, CA*
DESIGN • *Altoon + Porter Architects*

D/E/F: CRATE & BARRELL • *Stanford S/C, Stanford, CA*
DESIGN • *ELS*

A

B

C

D

E

F

A

B

Frank Gehry creates a new landmark on Dusseldorf's waterfront with a series of mirror-like shapes and forms that break out in bows and arcs and that throw warped reflections onto the neighboring structures.

This New York skyscraper—also facing the waterfront—has a half round, mirror finished facade that stands as a beacon on lower Broadway. It makes a tall, proud welcoming gesture. Shown here are several views of the building as seen approaching from uptown and heading to the tip of the island.

| A/B | FRANK GEHRY BUILDINGS • *Dusseldorf, Germany* |

| C/D/E: | NEW YORK, NY |

D

E

C

A

Colorado's Ocean Journey in Denver was created by Anderson Mason Dale Architects and RNL Designs as an aquarium. The lyrical waveform of the glass pavilion echoes the motion of water. The building's deck with cable rigging forms a metaphor for an ocean journey on a great ship. Playful sculptured forms are an abstraction of the under water world. The rich detailing of the brick assumes the character of Water Street architecture and recalls the Valley's great masonry tradition."

The Time Machine, designed by Cuningham Group, is curved to encompass a series of rides and exhibits that take in our travels through the centuries.

Greeting shoppers is the bold curved facade of Suadiye Department Store in Turkey designed by Kozu/Cirpici. The curved front is restated by the sharp horizontal shadows that delineate the telescoping upwards of the store's front design.

The horizontal banding is also stressed in the Rosslyn skyscraper. It is located just outside of Washington, DC. The semi-curved/semi-straight sided building is banded to emphasize that swing from the straight to the curved plane.

B

A/B:	COLORADO'S OCEAN JOURNEY • *Denver, CO*
C:	TIME MACHINE • *Seoul, Korea*
D:	SUADIYE DEPARTMENT STORE • *Turkey*
E:	ROSSLYN, VA

c

E

D

Sweeps, swells and in-viting curves appear in malls all around the world to draw shoppers off the aisles and into the open-for-viewing shops. Jean Claude Prinz of Paris, working for Oro Vivo has created this moving and sinuous shop front that appeared in a Neukirchen mall.

The MGM Grand shop and the Encompass store share the concept of a swelling, curved canopy/marquee that swings out over the shoppers in the aisles to ensnare them. The corner location of the MGM Grand shop makes full use of that sweep to carry the store's message to both traffic aisles. Encompass, designed by Michael Malone Architects, complements the bowed sign fascia with curved doors that carry through the in-viting movement.

B

C

| A/B: | ORO VIVO • *Neukirchen, Germany* |
| | PHOTO • *Gunther Binsack* |

| C: | MGM GRAND, *Las Vegas, NV* |

| D: | ENCOMPASS BY SHELL • *Dallas, TX* |
| | PHOTO • *Jud Haggard* |

D

Brick

A

Shown here are some "big box" type of stores that rely on the brickwork for the masonry. Brick is combined with stone, with wood, and with glass to create different overall looks from the warm and cozy, homey appeal of Kowalski's upscale market to the sophisticated look of the Follett College Book Store/Café. Ann Taylor's The Loft—an outlet store—goes "cozy" with the bright blue trim and the peaked wood outlined roof. The Athlete's Foot uses the red brick as a perfect foil for the company's bright yellow signature logo.

B

B

"brick: a hardened rectangular block of clay, dried and baked in a kiln. A building material that can be arranged in a variety of patterns and is also available in assorted earth colors—depending upon the clay used. The standard brick is 8 3/4" x 4 1/4" x 2 5/8" but can be ordered in different sizes and finishes."

B

E

A:	Larry's Shoes • *Denver, CO*
B:	Follett Book Store/Café Design • *AAD*
C:	Athlete's Foot Design • *Schafer Assoc.*
D:	Ann Taylor's The Loft Design • *Desgriuppes/Gobe Assoc.*
E:	Kowalski's Market Design • *KKE Architects*

A

Brick is earthy, hard but soft—and warm. It reminds us of hearth and home and when looking for a homey setting—and especially when selling food with "hearthy and hearty" appeal as in restaurants, grills and cafes—what could be more on-target than brick.

Illustrated here are some food venues: the very upscale and clubby The Clubhouse to a new hamburger place in Tokyo. There is the very friendly, inviting and traditional brickwork of Donato's Pizza designed by Chute Gerdeman to the striking pattern selected by GGLO for the facade of Torrefazione Italia. Here the contrasting colored bricks on the piers make the difference. The Clubhouse combines brick with elegant stonework and a classic cornice plus piers for its upscale standard.

The small, unpretentious streetside Streetside Seafood Café by JPRA Architects relies on the old brick facade painted a cool, fresh, sea-worthy aqua-green to make its point.

A: THE CLUBHOUSE • *Chicago, IL*
        DESIGN • *Jerry Knauer*

B: DONATO'S • *Reynoldsburgh, OH*
        DESIGN • *Chute-Gerdeman*

C: TORREFAZIONE ITALIA • *Seattle, WA*
        DESIGN • *GGLO*

D: MOS BURGER • *Tokyo, Japan*
        DESIGN • *Design Forum*

E: STREETSIDE SEAFOOD CAFÉ
        DESIGN • *JPRA Arch.*
        PHOTO • *Beth Singer*

D

C

B

C

B

A

To create a warm, inviting, village-like setting in a relatively sparsely settled part of Maryland, the designers wisely opted for brick and the Colonial vernacular for creating the look of River Village in Columbia, MD.

Brick is used to face the low buildings and even some of the paths that divide the shopping center up into "streets." Old fashioned light fixtures, planters, benches and trees all contribute to the nostalgic charm of the center and it imbues the various retail and commercial tenants with a sense of familiarity.

E

C

D

RIVER VILLAGE • *Columbia, MD*

Brickwork

B

A

More than bricks—it is what you do with them! On some of the previous pages we have pointed out the use of contrasting colored bricks to create different patterns. Here, we go back—quite a bit back in time—to show how some of the "old timers" a century or so ago-or early in the 20th century—used brick with imagination and style.

A/B:	BRUSSELS • *Belgium*
C:	SYDNEY B. • *9th Ave., Chelsea, New York, NY*
D:	MORGAN & CO. • *Westwood Village, Los Angeles, CA*
E:	KOBLIN'S PHARMACY • *Nyack, NY*

E

D

C

Canopy

Here are some bold—and one restrained—projections. The Oakland U.S. Ice Center boasts a giant sweep of bright red corrugated metal that spreads its wings over the entrance doors to the arena. The bright red complements the black and white stonework of the balance of the entrance design and the silvery metallic finish of the rest of the structure.

For the Hoyt Cinema facade, Thomas Bakalars swings a swoop of his own to create a bold facade statement and a covering for the patrons who have to wait to get into the cinema. Here, too, the stonework is patterned in contrasting colored stones and the red also becomes the signature color for the fin-like, vertical projection.

In a gentler statement, Brand + Allen's rehabbed building that serves as the home for Restoration Hardware, the original glass and steel framed canopy floats out over the entrance and show windows. The canopy is supported from metal rods anchored in the building.

A

C

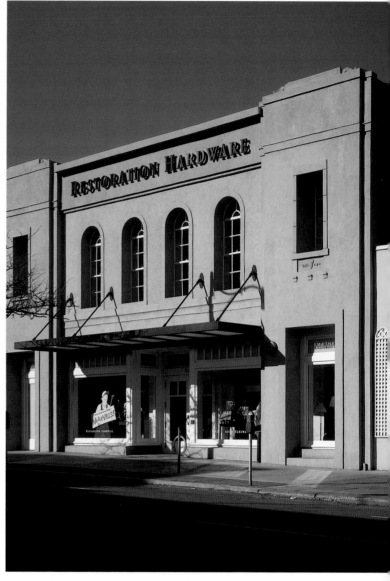

B

"canopy: an overhanging projection. A marquee. A free-flying, cantilevered shelf."

A/B:	OAKLAND U.S. ICE CENTER • *Oakland, CA* DESIGN • *Bottom Duvivier*
C:	HOYT'S CINEMA DESIGN • *Thomas Bakalars*
D:	RESTORATION HARDWARE DESIGN • *Brand + Allen*

Centro, a new giant retail and entertainment complex built in Oberhausen which is approximately 30 miles outside of Dusseldorf, Germany, was designed by RTKL Architects. It features skeletal steel and glass canopies that extend up and out over the building like Spanish combs awaiting mantillas to drop over them. The same metal and glass canopies are evident over and fronting the cafés and casual dining spots along the "street" where Entertainment reigns in Centro.

The new Joop! Shop in South Miami Beach is accented with a glass and metal framed canopy that steps out from the contemporary building's architecture. The curved front adds importance to the corner entrance as well.

The Library Café on Main St. in Venice, CA gains street prominence and also provides comfort for its outside seating with the wood grid canopy that is filled with panes of glass. The harmful sun's rays are held back while light still passes through.

A bold, pitched canopy steps out to greet shoppers to Nature's Northwest store. The apex of the triangular canopy is filled with glass panes which again fill the space below with light. The giant glass curtain wall, over the entrance doors, is also ready and willing to let light seep into the store.

A

B

48

A/B :	CENTRO • *Oberhausen, Germany* DESIGN • *RTKL Architects*
C:	JOOP! • *So. Miami Beach, FL*
D:	LIBRARY CAFÉ • *Main St., Venice, CA*
E:	NATURES NORTHWEST • *Lake Oswego, OR*

E

D

C

Classic Contemporary

A

B

Classic Greek and Roman architectural details updated and simplified to comfortably sit in modern day settings and even serve the high-tech needs of the public: Classic Contemporary.

Rodeo Drive is, once again, the place to find the classics revived and elegantly reinterpreted. There are the simple arches that provide a rhythmic softness, the columns capped with Ionic-like details that are more art deco than Greek, piers ending in moldings rather than flattened capitals and dentil molding added with flair. The Tommy Hilfiger store, on Rodeo Drive, sets a handsome example for others to follow.

A/B: **RODEO DRIVE** • *Beverly Hills, CA*
          DESIGN • *The Jerde Partnership*

C/D/E: **TOMMY HILFIGER** • *Rodeo Drive, Beverly Hills, CA*

C

D

E

E

More examples of the restrained classic elegance found on Rodeo Drive including the two-level Boss facade.

Nitya, in Paris, has a contemporary shop front design set into a classic Beaux Artes building but the two live comfortably and amicably—design wise.

For the Turnbull & Asser store on Madison Ave. the designers created this elegant, elongated store front that is classic in concept and in its use of the stone masonry. Even the incised name acknowledges the classic inspiration.

Willowbee & Kent, in Boston, retains its classic heritage. The updated triglyphs and metopes also suggest an art deco revival but the globe-lit torcheres to either side of the black enamel and brass accented entranceway are right out of the Forum.

A

C

D

A:	TURNBULL & ASSER • *Madison Ave., New York, NY*
B:	WILLOWBEE & KENT • *Boston, MA*
C:	RODEO DRIVE • *Beverly Hills, CA*
D:	BOSS • *Rodeo Drive, Beverly Hills, CA*
E:	NITYA • *Paris, France*

B

A

B

The Bellagio Hotel, in Las Vegas, reeks with the classics and the elegance of the 18th century Classic Revival. These decorative elements are redefined and refined for a new affluent society and the Hermes and Chanel shops are only two of the inside-the-shopping center facades that express the new contemporary classic look.

Mikimoto Pearls, located in the Shops of the Venetian Hotel in Las Vegas, plays with classical architectural elements to achieve a look that not only complements the hotel's theme but the image of the product.

In a more obvious manner the Hollywood & Grand shop in the MGM Hotel in Las Vegas really restates the classic motifs with blocks of masonry, the Greek key design under the neon sign, the ultra sized triglyphs and metopes and the simplified piers to either side of the entrance.

In Santiago, Corso Italia's faux marble facade and "masonry" more than imply the Roman styling of the fashions contained within.

E

C

D

A:	CHANEL • *Bellagio, Las Vegas, NV*
B:	HERMES • *Bellagio, Las Vegas, NV*
C:	CORSO ITALIA • *Santiago, Chile*
D:	HOLLYWOOD & GRAND • *MGM Hotel, Las Vegas, NV*
E:	MIKIMOTO PEARLS • *The Venetian, Las Vegas, NV*

Classic Floridian

A

B

There was a period in the 1920s and 1930s when the rich and the mighty "discovered" the southern part of Florida and began a building boom of Mediterranean-inspired palazzos and public buildings. This delightful mix of classic Italian motifs, Mediterranean-style red tile roofs, stucco finished facades and touches of the emerging art deco, all together blended with the blue skies, bluer water and the graceful royal palms. This sophisticated blend became the new architectural expression that was Floridian in nature. Mizner Park, a recent multipurpose development in Boca Raton, builds on that Classic Floridian tradition to become an upscale, fashionable setting for shops, cafés, offices and residences.

MIZNER PARK • *Boca Raton, FL*

C

E

D

F

Color

Boise Spectrum contains not only a vast range of retail shops, entertainment venues, restaurants and fun things to see and do but it also plays the gamut of color throughout the space. The many buildings are alive with rich, warm, earth-inspired colors that range from creamy yellows and golds to peach and salmon all the way to lavender, brick and terra cotta,. In addition, a multitude of bright accent colors add to the technicolor look of this out-of-doors mall. Art Moderne and Art Deco inspirations enliven the Edwards Megaplex and at night the brilliant rainbow of neon adds new excitement and even more color to this already colorful mall.

Boise Spectrum • *Boise Idaho*
Design • *Perkowitz + Ruth*
Photo • *Rick Keating*

B

A

C

D

E

A

Color makes a statement! It sets a mood—a look—and definitely has "attitude." Color is not for the mild or the meek. Color steps out from the building line with an in-your-face expression that says—"Here I am!"

Some examples of shopfronts that dare you to ignore them are shown on these pages. They range from the earthy gold colors of the Sun & Ski Sports stores to the flaming reds of Canal City and Model Zone. In keeping with the fun feeling

of Malibou Speed Zone, we see the bright chrome yellow facade of the Top Eliminator structure.

How can anyone resist the color sampler look of the Enterprise Pub in Camdentown, in London? With complete disregard to the architecture and to the period, but with complete accord with the place, the owners of the pub use color to say "Come and get it!." If the reader will turn to p. 150-151, he or she can see what some of the neighboring houses look like and perhaps better understand this color-filled expression.

B

A:	CANAL CITY • *Hakata, Japan*
	DESIGN • *The Jerde Partnership & Clifford Seibert*
B:	THE ENTERPRISE PUB • CAMDEN TOWN, LONDON, UK
C/D:	SUN & SKI SPORTS
	DESIGN • *Gottsdiner*
E:	MALIBOU SPEED ZONE • *Dallas, TX*
	DESIGN • *RTKL Assoc.*

C

D

F

E

A

C

BEMBO • *Downtown, Lima, Peru*

BEMBO • *Caminos del Inca, Lima, Peru*
DESIGN • *Jose Orrega Herrera*

B

RED! YELLOW! BLUE! How much more primary can you get!! There is nothing timid or retiring about these shop fronts designed by Jose Orrega Herrera of Lima, Peru for the Bembo chain of fast food restaurants in that busy, colorful, Latin American city.

Using bold, bright splashes of these colors broken into odd, angular shapes and juxtaposed with panes of glass caught in a web of black metal framework, each view of each store is a unique expression or a dimensional cubistic painting.

Illustrated here are two different locations and two different solutions for the same client.

D

E

Diners

A

B

The Star Diner, in Kentland S/C, in Maryland picks up the checkerboard pattern along with the Art Moderne design inspiration to recreate the by-gone look in a new open shopping center.

The Stardust Diner, in mid-town NYC—in the heart of the theater district, takes the subways that move underground as its inspiration for a "diner car" and carries the theme through with fun and imagination.

Located in a new, multi-purpose building in Garden City, NY is the Omni Diner designed by Mojo Stumer. Using all the nostalgic concepts and materials but targeted at a new generation of fast fooders, the Omni Diner creates the desired "old-fashioned" feeling in the sophisticated setting.

Whether they stand by the side of the road or the highway, or they are set down in mid-town, a diner is a diner and is usually recognizable as a diner. New or old, the diner has a look that is a nostalgic, backwards glance to the 1940s and 1950s—of Streamline Moderne—of glistening metal patterned in sunbursts—or corrugated, of neon and glass blocks.

Shown here are some different diner designs. Eat'n'Park, designed by Judd Brown Designs, is "traditional" in its use of glass, glimmer, and glitz and of neon and metal and the popular checkerboard pattern.

D

C

E

A:	Eat 'N' Park
	Design • *Judd Brown Designs*
B:	Star Diner • *Kentland S/C, Kentland, MD*
C/D:	Stardust Diner • *Broadway, New York, NY*
E:	Omni Diner • *Garden City, NY*
	Design • *Mojo Stumer*

Exotic

B

"Strange, exciting, glamorous" all describe and define Graumann's Chinese Theater on Hollywood Blvd. in Los Angeles. Not only does it make a striking appearance on a street full of strange and sometimes wondrous sights but it recalls the era of the Movie Palaces when they were built in exotic, romantic, and over-the-top styles that enhance the movie-going experience.

The Chinese Palace restaurant, in Centro, in Oberhausen, Germany recreates the architecture and look of a bye-gone period. The Chinese architectural and design elements—more realistic in interpretation than that of the Graumann's Theater—still are exotic and brings a faraway culture to the life of the German citizens who flock to Centro for their escape from their everyday Existences.

A

C

D

"exotic: of foreign origin or character; introduced from abroad. Striking or unusual in effect or appearance; strange, exciting, glamorous."

A/B:	CHINESE PALACE • *Centro, Oberhausen, Germany*
C/D:	GRAUMANN'S CHINESE THEATER • *Hollywood Blvd., Los Angeles, CA*

Fantasy

"fantasy: imagination, especially when exaggerated or unrestrained."

Shown here are some fantastic fronts—some are inside malls while others are out in the open—but all create indelible impressions.

With its profusion of foliage and overscaled, overstated animals and birds as well as textures galore, the Rainforest Café makes its presence noted in The Source, a mall located on Long Island in NY. The giant mushroom serves as a semi-outdoor café for this fun-oriented restaurant. The playful animals out front act as guides to the dining adventure that follows within.

Species Walk, created by MBH Architects, leaves civilization behind and invites visitors to trek through a fantasy jungle.

For the Universal Park in Orlando, FL, AAD created a series of unique and wildly imaginative shops that include the two shown here: Jurassic Park and Port of Entry. In both instances there is a basis in reality but then the designers' imagination takes off and soars. The only thing that holds these concepts earthbound is the engineering feat of construction.

For the Athletic Club at the MGM Grand in Las Vegas, JGA designed this exotic structure that starts off with an Indonesian inspiration that is soon transposed into the never-never fantasy land of a Las Vegas shopping strip.

A: RAINFOREST CAFÉ • *The Source, Westbury, NY*
     DESIGN • *Daroff Design*
     PHOTO • *Elliot Kaufman*

B: ENDANGERED SPECIES WALK
     DESIGN • *MBH Architects*

C: JURASSIC PARK • *Universal Park, Orlando, FL*
     DESIGN • *AAD*

D: PORT OF ENTRY • *Universal Park, Orlando, FL*
     DESIGN • *AAD*

E: MGM GRAND • *Las Vegas, NV*
     DESIGN • *JGA*

A

B

C

D

E

Foreign Places

E

You don't need a passport to travel to foreign places. All it takes is airfare to Las Vegas where the whole world has been encapsulated for your viewing pleasure. Visit Ancient Egypt, a Caribbean pirate port, the Paris of your dreams, Medieval England with knights on chargers—or see the wonders of Venice without the debris floating in the canals but still be careful of the pigeons or enjoy the exoticism of the East—"where the sun comes up like thunder" over Mandalay Bay.

Where The Venetian works at Disney-fying its vision of Venice, the canals, Str. Marks Square, the Palazzos and Piazzas Mandalay Bay creates a contemporized vision of that strange, exotic and faraway place.

A

B

C

A/B: Venetian • *Las Vegas, NV*

C/D/E: Mandalay Bay • *Las Vegas, NV*

D

Fun 'n' Funky

A

Some streets keep calling you back because there is always something old/new, weird/beautiful, fun/funky about them. Melrose Ave. in Los Angeles has its days—has its moments but it always has its share of in-your-face shopfronts that shock, surprise and often delight. Panache = Melrose Ave. Outrageous colors, indefinable surface treatments, and strange and conflicting fashion statements make this a streetscape like a trip to Alice's Wonderland where way-out shops and way-in dining spots mingle.

MELROSE AVE • *Los Angeles, CA*

B

C

D

E

F

Geometrics

D

More than simple vertical plinths or circular towers, these are facades that mix, match and meld triangles, rectangles, cylinders and other geometric shapes to create exciting and unique architectural statements.

Illustrated here is Rockenwagner, a museum located just off Main St. in Venice, CA. The design of Frank Gehry, it is a wondrous collection of oddly shaped rectangles that create an even more exciting play of shadows. The paint and metal sheathed surfaces interact in neutral shades of gray.

ROCKENWAGNER MUSEUM • *Venice, CA*
DESIGN • *Frank Gehry*

A

B

The Gap store on Collins Ave. in South Miami Beach combines a swelling gray form with vertical and angled cream colored rectangles to affect a most unusual and dramatic effect amid the Art Deco beauties on the street. The geometry is played out in the window openings and the vents on the left.

Simple, bold geometric forms are combined by Jose Orrega Herrera in the striking facade shown here. Bands of rough hewn stone in alternating rows of beige and gray flank the slick glass covered central block. A partial cylinder of glass breaks away from the block to create a welcoming entranceway.

The wall surrounding Sawgrass Mills S/C in Florida is all white and pierced with rectangles and circles.

The Convention Center in South Beach boasts a fabulous tower construction that looks like paper that has been folded, scored, and cut-out, to create a variety of shapes and patterns that move back and forth in all three planes.

A

B

E

A:	THE GAP • *Collins Ave., South Miami Beach, FL*
B:	BUILDING • *by J.Orrega Herrera of Lima, Peru*
C/E:	CONVENTION CENTER • *Washington Ave., South Miami Beach, FL*
D:	SAWGRASS MILLS • *S/C, Florida*

"geometric: resembling or employing the simple rectangular or curvilinear lines or forms used in geometry."

D

A

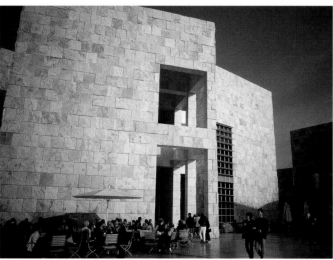

C

The Getty Museum, one of Los Angeles's newest attractions, is a wonderful display of geometric magic with cubes, blocks, rectangles, cylinders and other forms of all sizes and stone finishes combined with flair and daring. In every direction—wherever one looks—there is this exquisite balance of shapes and forms: all geometry and all spectacular. Adding to the ambiance are the greenery, the gardens, the expanses of glass, the terraces, the flights of steps, and the feeling of movement in these stationary, masonry constructions.

THE GETTY MUSEUM • *Los Angeles, CA*

E

F

B

D

Big Box stores and department stores are usually boxy and bulky. However, when designers rely on geometrics and play with shapes and forms, the overbearing volume of the box is cut down into more interesting and more human-scaled constructions.

Shown here are several department stores and also a big box store. By the use of blocks and forms and sometimes by cutting the volume with color changes, the results are exciting and inviting.

| A: | BETTER SPACES |
| | DESIGN • *Schafer Assoc.* |

| B: | PALACIO DE HERRA • *Mexico City, Mexico* |

| C: | WARDS |
| | DESIGN • *Shea Architects* |

D:	UPTON'S • *Snellville, GA*
	DESIGN • *Fitzpatrick Design Group*
	PHOTO • *Whitney Cox*

| E: | MAURI IMAI • *Tomakamai, Japan* |
| | DESIGN • *C&J* |

B

C

D

E

A

B

Geometric shapes + color! Shown here are some examples of the striking addition of accent colors to further break up the bulkiness of some buildings.

The Kenneth Cole store on Collins Ave. in South Beach and the Adidas Store in Portland both feature vertical pylons that serve as attention-getters and also contribute to the playful interchange of forms, shapes and planes.

Andronico's in the Stanford S/C uses the rich red rectangle not only to highlight the entrance into the upscale market in a very upscaled mall but it also relieves the blocks of light colored brick and the base of natural stone. From any view, that single form of color transforms the entire structure's design.

A:	ADIDAS, *Portland, OR* DESIGN • *Mobius*
B:	KENNETH COLE • *Collins Ave, South Miami Beach, FL*
C/D/E:	ANDRONICO'S • *Stanford S/C, Stanford, CA* DESIGN • *Sutti Architects*

C

E

D

Glass

Sheer curtain walls of glass that extend up two, three or more stories and open up the whole store to public viewing: that's Spectacle! Spectacular are these open facades garnered from New York, London and Sao Paulo.

Reiss' Men's Shop puts its almost all-white store on view in this wonderful, glass-ful facade expression where each floor becomes a display area. The lighting, up front in the window area, adds to the great look of the shop front.

The Swatch store on E.57th St. in New York City also opens up three stories for viewing. A giant Swatch watch fills the central glazed area of the two upper floors while the lower street level is divided up with display windows and the entrance doors.

Huis Clos, an exclusive designer's boutique in Sao Paulo, Brazil turns the high, narrow and beautifully designed store into a total showroom. The 20 ft. + windows soar uninterrupted to not only show off the main level but also to afford the passersby glimpses of the mezzanine located at the rear of the space.

A: REISS MEN'S STORE • *London, UK*

B: SWATCH, E.57TH ST • *New York, NY*

C: *(opposite page)*
       HUIS CLOS • *Sao Paulo, Brazil*
       DESIGN • *Studio Casas*

A

B

B

A: LACOSTE • *Costa Mesa, CA*

B: MARCCAIN • *Toronto, ON*
DESIGN • *ll X lV*

C: FOOT ACTION

D: LA PELLE • *Honolulu, HI*
DESIGN • *AM Partners*

E: EYEWORLD • *Bridgeside Galleria, MA*
DESIGN • *Bergmeyer Assoc.*
PHOTO • *Lucy Chen*

A

C

E

D

Sheets of glass can be angled to create gentle but definite directors. They lead the shoppers on the mall aisle or on the shopping street into the store's entrance which can be just an opening in the glass or a foyer-like space between the mall or street line and the store interior.

The Foot Action store subtly wends its way towards the store's opening while the other stores shown create dramatic pauses before the openings. Marccain, in Toronto, has a classic, symmetrical glass facade with the entrance dead center. The entrance to La Pelle is dramatized by a curved canopy that comes out between the-all glass side windows. La Coste, in Costa Mesa, depends upon the brushed steel base strips and the window frames to define the glass side windows. Eyeworld is also an all-glass expression but here the entrance is set off-center and this allows the designer to make interesting, asymmetrical use of the windows for product and brand displays.

Grids

Grids, in shop fronts or facades, are usually formed of metal or wood and inset with rectangular panes of glass. One these pages we show some exciting variations of grids used on buildings. The gridded glass partitions create the truly striking feature of the architectural design.

A/B:	COMMUNICATION CENTER • *Dusseldorf, Germany*
C:	ALL AMERICAN SPORTS • *Las Vegas, NV* DESIGN • *Swisher Hall* PHOTO • *Michaels*
D:	HOTEL • *South Miami Beach, FL*
E:	ARMANI • *Rodeo Drive, Beverly Hills, CA*

B

A

88

C

D

E

A

Grids or Grills—squared off and patterned!

B

The Fitzpatrick Design Group creates a dramatic glass tower as the corner entrance to the Maison Blanche store. The soaring atrium is captured in a grid of metal that rises up several stories to create an open space capped by a gridded glass ceiling. The side entrances are highlighted by glass filled gridded curtain walls between the expanses of masonry.

Elbasani & Logan Architects used an angled glass and steel grid to complement the fabulous wall of glass and metal framing that puts the Crate & Barrel store on view to the visitors to the Stanford S/C. The grid becomes the decorative motif that contrasts with the scale of the brick masonry and the rough, stone rubble construction.

Dunkin Donuts outlet in Lima gains street prominence with the red grid pattern that makes up the glazed areas of the facade. It highlights the corner entrance and the window areas to either side in the white stucco facade.

The Hollywood Galaxy Cinema on Hollywood Blvd. combines Streamline Moderne motifs with the grid pattern. The grid appears in the blue framed glass of the entrance cylinder, in the tile and the glass blocks as well as on the metal sheathed base of the structure.

A: HOLLYWOOD GALAXY • *Hollywood Blvd., Los Angeles, CA*

B: MAISON BLANCHE
        DESIGN • *Fitzpatrick Design Group*

C:/D: CRATE & BARREL STANFORD S/C • *Stanford, CA*
        DESIGN • *ELS*
        PHOTO • *David Wakely*

E: DUNKIN DONUT • *Lima, Peru*
        DESIGN • *J. Orrega Herrera*

D

E

C

A

B

Grids appear in malls where the sharp outline pattern may be all the decor that is needed. The metal grid can also be especially effective at night when the square frames grow in prominence thanks to the light emanating from the illuminated stores.

The Tower Records store in Lincoln Center in NYC truly comes alive at night. The store is on view through the gridded windows that extend up to the second level and across the Broadway expanse.

Boston Trading and Swing both rely on the sharp black boxes to make strong statements within the mall. Note how both repeat the grid as canopies overhead: in wood for Swing and black metal and glass for Boston Trader.

The W H Smith shop zigs and zags its way through the space making a striking design with the dark painted, shoji-like, framework.

"grid: a network of horizontal and perpendicular lines intersecting at right angles." A grillage or gridiron.

A:	W H Smith Design • *Brand + Allen*
B:	Tower Records • *Lincoln Center, New York, NY* Design • *Buttrick, White & Burtis* Photo • *Matt Wargo*
C:	Swing • *Miami, FL* Design • *Pavlik Design Group*
D:	Boston Trading • *Atlanta, GA*

C

D

High Tech

High Tech materials can be "futuristic"—"space age"—"urban"—"industrial." They can be used on store fronts to suggest a time, a place, a kind of product or service.

Panels of corrugated metal sheets can be as new and shiny as tomorrow or be used to recreate the look of diners of the '40s and '50s. Chute Gerdeman used the shiny corrugated material to create the facade for CV Wrappers in an active food court setting. However, the corrugated material has been aged and patinaed to create an old food stand in Hawaii for Maui Tacos.

The Big Entertainment open store front is accented by the textured metal panels that introduce the space age feeling of the store beyond.

The Kenneth Cole store takes on an urban attitude thanks to the I-beam construction that dramatically enhances the entrance into the Santa Monica shop. The same, rugged I-beam construction serves as the open facade for the Titanic exhibit in Paramount Park. The steely look has a strong and powerful presence in the entertainment venue.

A:	W H Smith
	Design • Brand + Allen
B:	Tower Records • Lincoln Center, New York, NY
	Design • Buttrick, White & Burtis
	Photo • Matt Wargo
C:	Swing • Miami, FL
	Design • Pavlik Design Group
D:	Boston Trading • Atlanta, GA

A

B

C

E

D

Illumination

Forget about lighting up the sky—illuminate the facade! Make it glow! Make it sparkle! Make it stand out in the night! Bathe it with warm lights that highlight the details and the architectural design. Make it come alive!

Shown here are department stores—some old like Debenham's in Leeds and some new like the Hyundai department store in Seoul. Some have just been given a new attitude so see what the nighttime illumination does for them.

B

A

D

C

A: NORDSTROMS
       DESIGN • Callison Architects
       PHOTO • Chris Eden

B: PACIFIC PLACE • Seattle, WA
       DESIGN • Elkus Manfredi

C: HYUNDAI DEPT. STORE • Seoul, Korea
       DESIGN • Pavlik Design Team

D: DEBENHAM'S • Leeds, UK
       DESIGN • Carte Blanche

E: CENTURY 21 • Westbury, NY
       DESIGN • FRCH

A

B

Lights—dazzling multi-color, technicolored lights: they are part of the entertainment scene. Neon, halides, wall washers, downlights, chasing lights: they go together to create the look and feeling of fun and excitement. Illustrated here are some of these color filled extravaganzas—all lit up!

C

D

E

A:	Ontario Mills • *CA*
B:	AMC • *Ontario Mills , CA* Design • *GB Designs*
C/D/E:	Grand Casino Tunica • *MS* Design • *Cuningham Group*

Kilowatts Up!

More colored lights and more lighting effects. From Circus Circus in Las Vegas to the ultra classy and classic Benaroya Hall in Seattle, it is the lighting effects that make the scene come alive. The Pacific Science Center, also in Seattle, takes on a unique glow when the sun sets and the kilowatts go up.

A/B:	PACIFIC SCIENCE CENTER • *Seattle, WA* DESIGN • *Callison Architects* PHOTOGRAPHER • *Chris Eden*
C:	BENAROYA HALL • *Seattle, WA* DESIGN • *LMN Architects*
D:	CIRCUS CIRCUS • *Las Vegas, NE* PHOTOGRAPHER • *J.F.Housel*

B

C

D

Kilowatts On

B

The Foot Locker stores, designed by Elkus Manfredi, reach out from the mall line with a bravura display of lighting that grabs shoppers in the mall and holds them captive. In addition to the excitement generated by the hundreds of bulbs dotting the fascia and the brilliant red back-lighting of the logo sign, there are the clever illuminated "score boards" hanging out over the traffic aisle that add extra sizzle to the store's presentation.

Red Devil BBQ, designed by Yabu Pushelberg, starts "cooking" out on the street in Neumarket in Toronto with lights blazing and burning through the darkness. Red Devil makes one helluva impression on the street.

Using assorted types of lights, the Gordon Biersch Brewery/Pub affects a welcoming entrance when the lights go down and the action starts. The neon striped fin—up above the pitched roof—creates a fanciful feeling for this café.

Picida, an elegant fashion shop in Tatui, Brazil lights up the night and the fascinating geometrics of the building's architecture created by Studio Casas. While the store windows glow below the up-lighting of the columns and on the assorted planes and levels of the structure adds stature to the retail shop.

A/B:	FOOT LOCKER • NJ
	DESIGN • *Elkus Manfredi*
C:	RED DEVIL BBQ • *Toronto, ON*
	DESIGN • *Yabu Pushelberg*
D:	GORDON BIERSCH BREWERY/ PUB • *Anaheim, CA*
E:	PICIDA • *Tatu , Brazil*
	DESIGN • *Studio Casas*

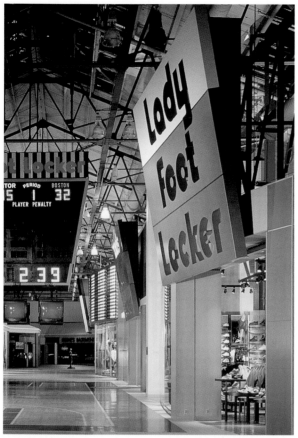

A

C

D

E

Lights Up

A

Bringing the store or the building into focus when day is done and the shopping still goes on, takes beacon-style illumination. Whether it is the store's interior—all lit up like the proverbial Christmas tree—or the facade accented by wall washers, up-lights, down-lights, goose neck extended fixtures or halide floods—it takes light to do it.

Woodwind & Brasswind, by Schafer Associates, not only is all lit up and aglow but extra attention has been paid to the pool in front and the overscaled musical instrument "sculpture" that serves as the dimensional logo for the store.

Where the Nike store's lighting, in Triangle Square, is soft and hazy and mostly due to the light reflected from behind the coves, Haggar's lettering on the brick facade is brightly and boldly illuminated by the goose-neck lamps that compliment the shop front design.

Two big, high-powered lamps light up the Kenneth Cole facade in Santa Monica. The golden yellow facade suggests some of the warmth that the indoor lighting guarantees.

B

| A/B: | WOODWIND & BRASSWIND |
| | DESIGN • *Schafer Associates* |

C:	NIKE • *Triangle Square*
	DESIGN • *Altoon + Porter Architects*
	PHOTO • *Paul Beilenberg*

| D: | KENNETH COLE • *Santa Monica, CA* |
| | DESIGN • *Akar Studio* |

D

E

C

A

Let it glow! Let it glow! Let it glow!—and glow it does. Times Square in New York City is all aglow with moving shapes and shadows, with images and messages, with colored lights changing the building architecture and effectively camouflaging most of it. At night there is no brick, no stone, no wood or glass—there are only the lights that take over and recreate the shop fronts and facades.

The Marketplace at the Millennium Center in Greenwich—just outside of London, England—is all aglow due to the lights that illuminate the dynamic, futuristic superstructure that hovers over the store located under the Millennium Dome.

Borders Book store in San Francisco glows at night with lights that wash over the building's "antique" architectural details and the seasonal banners that decorate and add color during the daylight hours.

A/B/C:	TIMES SQUARE • *New York, NY*
D: UK	THE MARKETPLACE • *Millennium Dome, Greenwich, London,* DESIGN • *RPA*
E:	BORDERS BOOK STORE • *San Francisco, CA* DESIGN • *FRCH*

E

B

C

D

Marquees

During the 1920s and 1930s, when movie palaces were proliferating, the marquee standing out from the building line not only made a strong presence on the street but protected the theater-goers from the change of weather. They also carried the information as to what was playing. That tradition extended into the Streamline Moderne cinemas of the 1940s. The marquee at the Trocadero, in Piccadilly Circus in London carries forward the same tradition as does the marquise vitree that serves as a herald and street sign for Macy's Sport store located one flight down in Macy's flagship store in Herald Square in New York City.

In malls, where the mall line can present a design barrier for the designer, the overhanging canopy or marquee may offer a way to gain store name or brand name recognition. Tapper's projects a giant grid out over its entrance while Braemar makes up in height for what it may lack in depth. The scalloped canopy carries the flowers and sail-like shapes that define Bittersweet and also introduces the store's logo elements. All are illuminated and all light up the entrances below.

A

B

C

E

A:	TROCADERO • *London, UK*
	DESIGN • *RTKL Assoc.*
	PHOTO • *Whitcomb*

B:	MACY'S HERALD SQUARE • *New York, NY*
	DESIGN • *Chute Gerdeman*

C:	TAPPERS
	DESIGN • *JGA*

D:	BRAEMAR • *Oakville Pl , Toronto, ON*
	DESIGN • *M. Hirschberg Design*

E:	BITTERSWEET • *Toronto, ON*
	DESIGN • *Candeloro Designs*

" marquee or marquise: a projection or canopy over a door or entrance." It is often decorative and was, in the 19th century, usually a glass and metal frames unit. The classic ones are often referred to as "marquise vitree,"

D

Metal Pipes

A

Pipes and pipe constructions add a fresh, high-tech and urban look to a shop front or facade. It is like a work in progress.

The Karstadt department store building in Hamburg gets a sporty new look with the addition of the metal pipe armature that runs up the sides of the structure and also acts as a support for the glass wall that steps away from the building line. The motif continues up on the roof and on the superstructure that houses a miniature sports arena.

In creating the open-to-the-skies Warringah Mall, Altoon + Porter used pipes of various thicknesses to create this high-tech yet user-friendly and comfortable setting. Pipes outline pipes, pipes hold pipe arches and even the glass enclosed, pitched roofs are encased and outlined with pipes.

The Hollywood Entertainment Museum uses the geodesic pipe armature to encase the structure and also to support the floating roof. The entrance to the museum is all glass block and recalls the art moderne style of the 1940 movie houses.

A:	KARSTADT SPORTHAUS • *Hamburg, Germany*
B:	WARRINGAH MALL DESIGN • *Altoon + Porter Architects*
C/D:	HOLLYWOOD ENTERTAINMENT MUSEUM • *Hollywood Blvd.,* *Los Angeles, CA*

C

B

D

Metallic Surfaces

B

A

Slick, shiny surfaces that pick up light and then reflect it—twist and turn it—can provide smart, contemporary shop front finishes. The metal sheet sheathing can reflect mirror-like or distort the reflections—can wrap around curves or provide a smooth glistening surface. Whether it is the copper sheeting used on the fascia of China Inn or the textured, Questech metal finish used on Frederick's or the subtle, satiny finish of Dune or the Richard Booth's shop fronts—the metallic finish adds to the sophisticated look of the store and its product.

A:	CHINA INN • *San Diego, CA*
	DESIGN • *Akar Studio*
B:	RICHARD BOOTH • *Toronto, ON*
	DESIGN • *II X IV Design*
C:	DUNE • *London, UK*
	DESIGN • *Skakel & Skakel*
D:	FREDERICKS

E

C

D

Mirror Images

B

Mirror like sheathing on skyscrapers, creates wonderful vistas of buildings on buildings and makes for whole new city streetscapes for anybody who is willing to look up to enjoy the spectacle.

Shown here are some skyscrapers in Chicago's financial district and the unusual, circular State Building that is also located in this area. The glass and metal finishes and the treatment of the glass altogether create these mirror-like surfaces.

A:	STATE BUILDING • *Chicago, IL*
B:	HOLLYWOOD & VINE • *Los Angeles, CA*
C:	IN LAND STEEL BUILDING • *Chicago, IL*
D:	FIRST NATIONAL BANK • *Chicago, IL*

D

A

C

Frank Gehry Buildings • *Dusseldorf, Germany*

Frank Gehry's cluster of modern buildings along Dusseldorf's waterfront are not only filled with the movement of undulating planes and arcs, bends and bows—like the water that runs nearby—but the skin of the buildings is highly polished, mirror-like sheets of metal applied to reinforce the unending movement and to catch the reflection of the surrounding buildings. As the sun moves or as the viewer's position changes so do the images reflected in the multi-planed, multi-storied, mirror finished buildings.

D

B

C

Neon

How better to light up the night and accentuate the shopfront or building than with ribbon streamers of brilliant neon? Ribbons of the bright, burning colors that can flash on and off or sizzle endlessly, play patterns in synch with a computer keyboard or just simply outline, underline or highline shapes and forms for the fun of it: that's what neon can do.

Bar Code is a new blazing addition to the Times Square Battle of the Neon Signs and the sharp blue neon stripes really tell the Bar Code story while making its strong presence felt on the already brilliantly-illuminated street. Almost next to it is the Virgin store where the red neon bars build up only to vanish and then build up again to another red block of color over the Sony Theater Cinemas sign.

Cinemas—especially those located in entertainment centers or malls—have joined in the contest. Shown here is the Embarcadero Center Cinema in San Francisco and the Warner Bros. theater in Centro, in Oberhausen, Germany

B

A

E

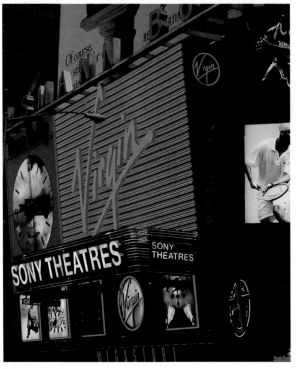

A: EMBARCADERO CENTER CINEMA • *San Francisco, CA*
          DESIGN • *ELS Architects*
          PHOTO • *John Sutton*

B: WB THEATER • *Centro, Oberhausen, Germany*
          DESIGN • *RTKL Assoc.*

C: BAR CODE • *Times Square, New York, NY*

D/E: VIRGIN RECORDS/SONY THEATER • *Times Square, New York, NY*

D

Night and Day

A

Business is no longer from sun-up to sunset. Not only are the business hours longer but retailers and manufacturers use the nighttime to reinforce and to further promote brand names and brand images. For the next several pages we are showing a series of malls, shopping centers, department stores, specialty stores and restaurants as they appear during the daylight hours and also the magical transformation that takes place when the sun goes down and the millions of kilowatts of light go on.

We start with the Palm Beach Mall designed by Pavlik Design Team and the Paramount Plaza—a renovation of an existing Midtown New York City space as accomplished by FRCH. Without changing the building's architecture, FRCH had to create a carnival-like excitement that would be able to stand up to and compete with the throb and tempo that surrounds this plaza on Broadway in the theater district.

B

A/B: PALM BEACH MALL • *FL*
        DESIGN • *Pavlik Design Team*

C/D/E: PARAMOUNT PLAZA • *Broadway, New York, NY*
        DESIGN • *FRCH*

C

D

E

A

B

C

D

The Cuningham Group's Time Machine not only attracts thousands of entertainment starved, satisfaction seekers to its doors by day but this entertainment venue functions well into the evening hours for the scores upon scores who line up to travel back to the past—and into the future.

In Hawaii, Altoon + Porter Architects created the Kaahumanu Center as an outdoor mall. At night, with lights ablaze, the unique circular structure rises up out of the darkness and beckons revelers and shoppers alike to venture forth and enjoy the delights contained within.

A/B:	TIME MACHINE • *Seoul, Korea* DESIGN • *Cuningham Group*
C/D:	KAAHUMANU CENTER • *Honolulu, HI* DESIGN • *Altoon + Porter Arch.* PHOTO • *David Franzen*

A

B

REI's glass tower that encloses the giant climbing wall takes on a new look at night when the light show actually begins and the rock pinnacle that has become a new Seattle landmark—and tourist attraction—is bathed in light and the store's logo lights up like a beacon

Azie is a new restaurant designed by Cass Caulder Smith. Located on Folsom St. in San Francisco in a rehabbed building, by day one can't help but be attracted by the clever collection of earth-toned cubes and the curtain wall of glass—all cleverly updated. At night the hot reds, golds and ambers spill out through the wide open glazed area to paint the street with their inviting and tantalizing warmth. Azie becomes the place to be!

A/B:	REI • *Seattle, WA* DESIGN • *Mithun Partners*
C/D/E:	AZIE • *San Francisco, CA* DESIGN • *Cass Caulder Smith*

D

E

B

A

Bloomingdale's department store in Aventura has a remarkable glass curtain wall that during the day filters out the sun's hot rays but allows the daylight to pass on through. The silvery, glassy look is cool and refreshing. At night, the light from inside the store comes out and turns the curtain wall into a live, glowing cube.

In Edinborough the HMV Music store shows its age. It is located in a period building on a street filled with other handsome, old structures of another century. At night, the "old girl's" wrinkles disappear and though the magic of flattering colored lights and boldly illuminated bold graphics—the "antique" is as young and sassy, as vivacious and funloving—as the young clientele that fills the store.

C

D

E

| A/B: | BLOOMINGDALE'S • *Aventura, FL* |
| | DESIGN • *Robert Young Assoc.* |

| C/D/E: | HMV MUSIC EDINBOROUGH • *Scotland, UK* |

A

The Malibu Speed Zone in Dallas is a day-into-night sort of entertainment venue. When the kids and their families leave at dusk, it is the teenagers, the 20-yr. olds and the young 30s that come flocking to enjoy the auto theme fun of Malibu Speed Zone. The fresh "cartoon" colors of daylight are turned into more sensual and emotional things by the nighttime lighting.

The CocaCola Pavilion in Atlanta is a big tourist attraction, and even when the doors are shut at night—the show goes on. The illumination fills the space and continues to "sell" the name and the product from dusk till dawn.

B

A/B: MALIBU SPEED ZONE • *Dallas, TX*
       DESIGN • *RTKL Assoc.*
       PHOTO • *Craig Blackman*

C/D: COCACOLA PAVILION • *Atlanta, GA*
       DESIGN • *TSVA*

C

D

A

B

Wyland Galleries facade is cool and all turquoise and marine blue during the daylight hours. The family of dolphins frolic in the gurgling pool out front. At night, a golden glow is cast over the setting and the fascia turns sea green and the illuminated sculptured dolphins in the pool turn gold and add to the magic of the space.

The CAT Merchandise Center in Peoria looks very much like a retail store on the ground level of an office building. The high-tech, CAT logo sign, over the entrance is all that distinguishes the store. However, at night, the CAT sign literally jumps off the building and the Merchandise Center marquee is completely lit up and the neon bands take over to accentuate the marquee over the entrance. To either side, up-lights and downlights add color to the store's front.

A/B: WYLAND GALLERIES
       DESIGN • *JGA*

C/D: CAT MERCHANDISE CENTER • *Peoria, IL*
       DESIGN • *Retail Design Group*

C

D

A

Eat'N'Park is a new "classic diner" (see "Diners") designed by Judd Brown Designs. It makes effective use of all the cliches of the '40s and '50s diner but in a new, fun way. Colored neon outlines the rooftop and the letters on the semi-circular marquee. BUT, it takes night time and light up time for the Eat'N'Park diner to really make its appearance as the neon brilliance intensifies and the quilted pattern on the metal sheathing picks up and reflects lights coming from passing cars and myriad other sources.

| A/B: | EAT 'N' PARK |
| | DESIGN • *Judd Brown Designs* |

C/D/E:	MONTERREY • *Royal Park, IL*
	DESIGN • *JPRA Architects*
	PHOTO • *Mitchell Kearney*

B

The Monterrey Café in Royal Park presents a happy face to the public with its bright green shop front adorned with eight ft. tall jalapegnos. The brickwork of the facade has been painted over with a creamy color and a giant red/ red violet sun-like orb dominates. Barely discernable are the neon jalapegnos over the awning. When the sun sets, Monterrey's "sun" lights up and makes a brilliant focal point on the painted facade. The neon outlined jalapegnos step forward. The down-lights, over the dimensional red hot peppers on the green wall, bring them into focus and into the diner's attention.

D

E

C

Quaint

A

B

Quaint is charming and "quaint" reminds us of "the good old days." Quaint is history—it is heritage—it is tradition and it offers us an escape from our high-tech, speed oriented, computerized and electronically controlled environments.

Many small, sleepy, almost forgotten towns are suddenly awakening to the throngs of visitors weary of their 21st century surroundings and looking for the peace and charm of a slower, more casual time. They are searching for Yesterday. Nyack, NY and Chester, NJ, are only two of these little rediscovered towns and their funny, old-fashioned architecture is being reevaluated and being appreciated. Without too much "dressing up" or too much "renovation"—these towns look and feel much as they did decades and decades ago.

For designers looking to create an immediate appeal for hand crafted, homemade or innocent and pure products or brand images—Quaint should do it!

D

C

A/B:	CHESTER • *NJ*
C/D/E:	NYACK • *NY*

"quaint: having an old fashioned charm or attractiveness."

E

BELLEVUE AVE. AND SPRING ST. • *Newport, RI*

Newport, RI is another historic city that enjoys being quaint. They revel in and are only to happy to share with visitors their quaint, period houses and shops—many that hark back to the 19th century. Even the "new" buildings that go up are based on the architectural styles that dominate the city's streetscapes and a pleasant patina of charm blankets the area.

D

B

C

A

Illustrated here are some current shop fronts and facades where the designers borrowed freely from the past to achieve a recognizable tie-in with "the good old days" when craftsmanship and values really counted for something.

The Andronico's Market relies on brick masonry and small gabled windows to affect a more Colonial look that will support the store's concept of value and quality.

For the Bear Village shop, Pavlik Design Team also relied on charm and quaintness as they created this old-fashioned shop front with gabled roof and mullioned windows. The

B

D

C

Rehabs

A

As a follow-up to "Quaint" what could be more appropriate than "Rehab." Don't tear down the past! Don't destroy the tradition and heritage! Build on them—enhance them—fix them and make them work again for the future while serving as a memorial to the past.

In the old downtown district of Pasadena is One Colorado: a new/old conglomerate of shops, restaurants and places of entertainment. The old brick factory buildings and warehouses of the early part of the 20th century now serve the young fun seekers for the 21st century.

They revel in the quaintness and the old fashioned quality of the uninspired architecture that has withstood decades of time but now is a Mecca for pleasure. Plants, trees, benches, colorful awnings, outdoor dining set-ups and amusing sculptures all make this rehabilitated cluster of buildings a destination to see and be seen in Pasadena,

B

ONE COLORADO • *Pasadena, CA*

D

C

E

A

The new REI flagship store designed by Mithun Partners is located in a rehabbed 1901 Denver Tramway Power Co. building. In keeping with REI's corporate passion and philosophy, the firm worked with the Landmark Preservation Commission and the Historical Society to " create a design which translated these values into a structure emulating the REI spirit while meeting strict historic guidelines."

The load bearing, brick powerhouse is Late Victorian in architectural style with Richardsonian Romanesque elements. The new materials that were used are compatible to the original and they were incorporated in as close to a "raw state" as possible. "The architecture focuses on structure, connections, how things are made, and the gentle inclusion of REI within the historic concept."

The project also preserves the character of the building's former use and the character of the internal volume. "There is a definite sense of the outdoor environment in the building's preserved volumes, natural light and 'character' of the spaces."

Because the building is located at the gateway to the central business district of Denver, parking is underground and there is a landscaped courtyard above with the building's foreground open to the south. "Out of respect for the historic structure and the neighborhood's diverse character, the native Colorado landscaped areas serve as a public green space."

B

REI • *Denver, Colo*
DESIGN • *Mithun Partners*

Spectaculars

Not simple statements but massive overstatements. Not realism but super realism. Spectacular means " dramatic, daring, thrilling." Spectacular is "impressive large scale displays." What these facades and shop fronts, and those on the following pages, have in common is that they are "impressive," "dramatic" and decidedly eye-filling!

It wouldn't be Planet Hollywood if it didn't overflow and overwhelm the street on which it was situated. The facade treatment of the Chicago Planet Hollywood is bold, big and very impressive. It impresses by its sheer volume and the brilliance of its color and the outrageous design.

A

B

D

In the Forum, in Las Vegas where everything is spectacular, one just can't be shy and retiring—or modest. So, the entrance to The Race to Atlantis, a popular thrill ride, comes rushing up at the visitor with Neptune and the sea monsters pulling his chariot up from the depths ready to engulf and overwhelm the attendee. The gold-tipped waves are certainly not understatements.

RA, a nightclub in the Egyptian-themed Luxor Hotel in Las Vegas makes its opening statement with the over-sized silver-plated, Amazon guards that stand to either side of the faux stone masonry. The Ra logo is brilliant in color and light.

A:	RACE FOR ATLANTIS • *The Forum, Las Vegas, NV*
B:	RA, LUXOR HOTEL • *Las Vegas, NV* DESIGN • *Dougall Design*
C/D/E:	PLANET HOLLYWOOD • *Chicago, IL*

E

C

Overscaled symbols, decorative, or logos all add up to spectacular facade presentations. The giant M&M package fills up three stories of the Ethel M Chocolate store in Las Vegas. The smiling, full round M&Ms are at least ten foot tall and that's a lot of chocolate! Against the blue/green-mirrored glass of the facade, these 3D units really pop out in a pop-out kind of city.

Let's go to the movies and as always—they are bigger than life. The entrance to the Hollywood Wax Museum consists of a giant spool of film unwinding to become the ticket booth. In Seattle, the Blockbuster store does it with a version of a streamline, '40s movie marquee that almost overwhelms the shop below. King Kong is alive and well—or at least exists in two dimensions as he hangs off the Suncoast Movie shop and the Sam Goody store on the Universal City Walk.

It is not an understatement when Club Disney offers fun within. Everything is big and bold: the checkerboard patterns, the stars, the moon, the forms and shapes.

A

B

D

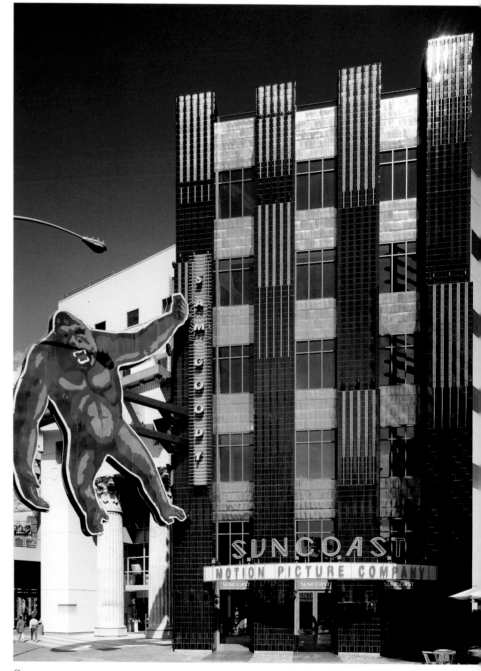

C

E

Superscale

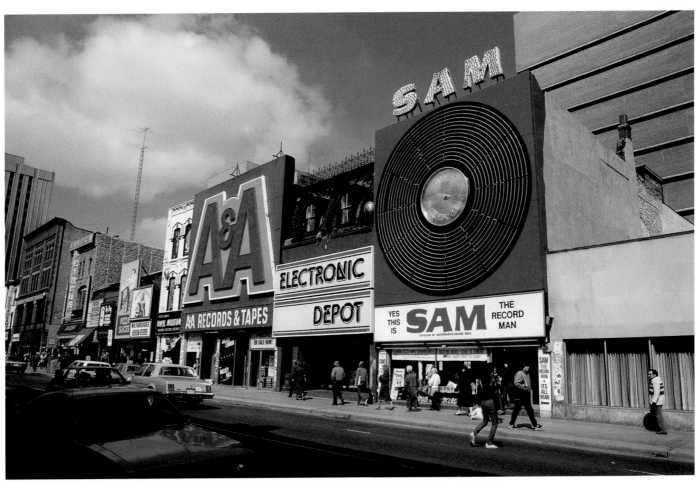

A

Here the emphasis is on size! Bigger is better! On a street where everybody is yelling and flaunting their goods, Sam out-flaunts them with his giant record that tells anyone within streets of the store that this is the place for Records and CDs. Sam does get some competition from A&A who also has discs to sell and is not keeping it a secret.

The Planet Hollywood in Centro Mall, in Oberhausen, is filled with overstatements and the biggest and boldest is the zebra pattern that serves to highlight the fascia. Note the King Kong painting that fills the tower over the entrance.

It's the giant spoon and the equally overstated red and white checkerboard pattern that makes the Betty Crocker stand stand out in the mall.

As a real water tower or beer vat this one wouldn't be so big but as decorative signage the simulated beer vat at Gordon Biersch Brewery/Café and the aluminum sheathed tower atop Deep Denim make big statements on the street.

B

A:	Sam's • *Yonge St., Toronto, ON*
B:	Planet Hollywood • *Centro, Oberhausen, Germany*
C:	Betty Crocker • *Mall of America, Bloomington, MN*
D:	Gordon Biersch Brewery/Pub • *San Francisco, CA* Design • *Allied A&D*
E:	Deep Denim • *Collins Ave., So., Miami Beach, FL*

E

C

D

Super Signage

When the signage dominates the façade; then it is Super Signage. When a whole district of tired, worn-down and uninspired early 20th century buildings becomes THE shopping street that appeals to the young—the fashion formers and reformers—the trendy and the way-out—then something has to give. What "gives" is the spectacular display of three dimensional elements, logos and signs that jump off the old buildings that are, in some cases, freshened up with coats of paint in bright and uninhibited colors with wild and crazy awnings to match. Camden Town, a northern outpost of London, beckons with sales of outrageous designs, second hand wares and ethnic food shops all presented amid the flurry of superimposed signs and fun statements.

A

CAMDEN TOWN • *London, UK*

B

C

D

E

F

Trompe L'Oeil

E

Illustrated on the following pages are two buildings—one an apartment building in downtown Portland and the other a restaurant in Las Vegas. What unites them is the unbelievable use of trompe l'oeil artwork on the relatively unadorned flat facades of the structures.

In the Portland building, dramatic and heroic scaled grisaille "sculpture" and architectural motifs are rendered with shadows on the flat surfaces of the building till it becomes monumental in appearance. The bowed areas are actually flat. The classic ornamentation and the window treatments on the upper story and the "cornice" are all artwork. The colonnade on the lower level is also accomplished with the monochromatic painting technique much favored in the late 18th century. It is painted on to the flat tiled area set into the building's brickwork.

"trompe l'oeil: French for deceive the eye. Objects rendered foreshortened and with shadows to appear three dimensional or real."

C

PORTLAND, OR

E

D

Sfuzzi, located on Las Vegas Blvd., is a true trompe l'oeil design–from all of the Venetian style arches and the art-work that seems to be peeling off of the building to reveal a solid brick surface below to the Mona Lisa framed painting superimposed over another part of the building. Note how the "hand" is pulling off the sheet of trompe l'oeil artworked facade to reveal the bare bricks beneath. What makes this type of facade such a delight is that the street viewer can't just pass it by but must stop and study it and maybe even get close enough to feel it and be sure that what seems to be there really isn't there. Adding to the "deception" in the Sfuzzi facade is the actual dimensional moldings, piers and arches that are mixed in with the deceptive ones.

SFUZZI • *Las Vegas Blvd., Las Vegas, NE*

F

C

E

Trompe l'oeil becomes street art and street theater when it not only creates a feeling of depth and dimension but also tickles the viewer's fancy.

Loew's wasn't going to rebuild the old brick warehouse in Cambridge that was going to house its new multiplex. Instead, using talented trompe l'oeil artists, they fashioned a grand and spectacular architectural facade that could have graced one of the Movie palaces of the 1920s or 1930s. Only the marquee actually steps out from the building line.

The little B&B in Madrid wasn't going to tell any of its possible guests that there were no windows in their rear rooms. So someone painted them in and even playfully raised or lowered louvered shades and pulled back imaginary curtains and drapes. The flowers on the balcony never need to be watered. The almost photographically rendered band across the building serves as an ad for the artists.

An old jumble of wood, brick and corrugated metal pieces make up the back of the New Orleans Jazz club. In the spirit of fun and the jazz music played within, an artist has interpreted it in this humorous and playful rendition of New Orleans architecture. It makes the back end of the structure almost as inviting as the entrance up front.

The Lincoln Building, in Washington, DC, adapts the art deco and art moderne architectural motifs that enrich the front facade and takes artistic liberties with them on the flat and unadorned side of the building. The artists have added pilasters, cut-outs, frames and even lanterns—in trompe-l'oeil—to turn the flat embarrassment into a three dimensional vision.

The 1920-ish stucco building that houses Nicole's Café in Frederick, MD get an architectural face-lift with a giant, trompe l'oeil mullioned window that opens up one side of the building. A bird flies out leaving its shadow behind on the painted surface.

D

D

F

A:	LOEW'S THEATER • *Cambridge, MA*
B:	BED & BREAKFAST • *Madrid, Spain*
C:	JAZZ CLUB • *New Orleans, LA*
D:	LINCOLN BLDG. • *Washington, DC*
E:	NICOLE'S CAFÉ • *Frederick, MD*

Vertical Statements

A

Vertical statement usually serve as exclamation points! They emphasize—they stress—they alert the public to something of importance and stature. Vertical lines mean power and strength. They are ' masculine" and also suggest dignity.

Shown here are some of the effective vertical statements that are lined up in the Chicago business district. They were built between 1950 and 1970 and are the works of some of the world's leading architects. Repetitive vertical masonry helps to make these structures seem even taller and even when horizontal bands are introduced, like in the 1st National Bank building, the verticality of the design does not yield. The Chicago Title & Trust building seems to consist of three vertical elements pushing upward and that vertical line continues up to the three screened towers that bring the line to its finale.

Also included is a business building in Rosslyn, VA.—just outside of Washington, DC. The curved, eyebrow-like canopies that extend out over the top don't really stop the dramatic repetition of the vertical lines that pattern the structure.

B

A:	55 W. MONROE ST. • *Chicago, IL*
	ARCHITECT • *Helmut John*
B:	BUILDING IN ROSSLYN • *VA*
C:	CHICAGO TITLE & TRUST • *Chicago, IL*
D:	1ST NATIONAL BANK • *Chicago , IL*

C

D

A

The Port Authority Building in Camden, NJ relies on the yellow painted columns on the lower two floors and on the upper stories to create the tall feeling desired. The decorative black and white banding plays off of the yellow enameled columns and colonnade on top that seems to push the roof up even higher.

The Venetian Hotel in Las Vegas—once one gets above the pseudo St. Marks Square architecture—consists of tall, sweeping lines that move ever upward. The arches on top recall the Venetian architectural motifs at street level.

Mandalay Bay may be exotic but it is also a hotel with lots and lots of rooms. To house them, the designers have created a multi-storied, contemporary building where the repeated emphasis on the vertical line seems to make the building soar upwards.

B

A/B:	Port Authority Building • *Camden, NJ*
C:	Venetian Hotel • *Las Vegas, NV*
D:	Mandalay Bay • *Las Vegas, NV*

C

D

Wall Art

Wall art is street art—not necessarily graffiti. It is there for the amusement, the entertainment and the pleasure of people on the street and often to relieve the utter boredom of a blank wall—one just begging to be scrawled on with paint cans.

As part of a community effort in Columbus to improve the looks of the neighborhood, retailers and restaurateurs undertook this art effort to make parking areas less of an eye sore. In one parking lot a history of train travel unwinds along the backs of unrelated but connected buildings. In another a classic train station, complete with arched openings and passengers running in and out, adds excitement to what would ordinarily be a blank experience—or worse. Note how the trees, plants and planters all contribute to the gracious feeling.

B

A

162

C

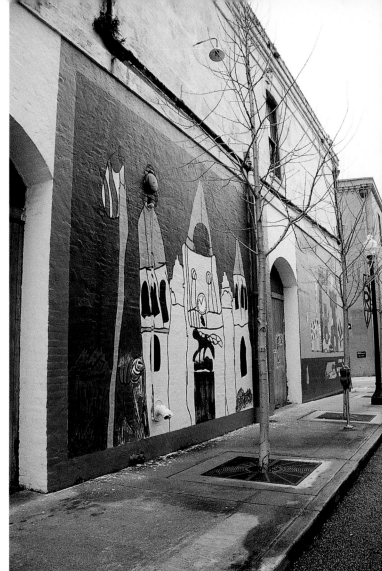

D

In New Orleans a rather bucolic setting surrounds two sides of a parking lot. Note how the live tree has been incorporated into the greenery of the artwork.

Down another street in New Orleans one can enjoy these murals on the walls of a reclaimed factory building which are based on children's artwork. The otherwise unpainted and unadorned rehabbed building was ripe for an attack by graffiti artists but what held them at bay was the respect for the artwork that offers so much visual pleasure to the people who live and work in this reclaimed area.

A/B:	*Columbus, OH*
C/D/E:	*New Orleans, LA*

E

B

B

A/B:	*Venice, CA*
C:	AIR SPORTS SPORTS CENTRE • *Toronto, ON*
D:	STILL LIFE CAFÉ • *Fremont, WA*
E:	SAN TELMO • *Buenos Aires, Argentina*

Main St. in Venice—California that is—is a street filled with fun and fanciful shopfronts and vintage facades. Adding to the good natured, easy going attitude of the community is this wall of strollers and shoppers that is painted to look like what Venice must have looked like a half century ago when what is now retro was actually new.

Wall Art becomes the striking storefront treatment for the Air Canada Center's sports store. The strong, dynamic and richly colored graphic sets the theme for the shop and provides the enticement to enter.

Wall Art comes in many forms and shapes and here is an expression found in a roll-down metal door in Buenos Aires. The Still Life Coffee Shop may be around the corner but the wall painting suggests that the trip will be worth it.

B

B

B

Wood

B

B

Along with stone, wood is one of Man's oldest building materials. Nothing recreates the sense of time past and of a bye-gone era like the use of wood: weathered, worn, shingled, stained or detailed with beveled panels and enriched with moldings.

The Harp Bar recalls what we think an Irish pub might look like in some local neighborhood in Dublin even though this one serves the hurrying commuters on their way to and from Penn Station in midtown Manhattan.

In keeping with the historic quality of Newport, RI (see "Quaint" p. 136-137) this harborside streetscape—not old but made to look old—is filled with fascinating uses of wood in various forms to create the tradition and ambiance of a century or more ago.

B

B

B

Twigs, in Nyack, NY (see 134-135) complements the vintage buildings of the village and this old/new shopfront is rich in nostalgia. he weathered finish adds to the "authenticity."

The red stained, wood faced building in Bristol, RI also recalls a bye-gone era and it is compatible with the surrounding old buildings.

A/B:	WHARF • *Newport, RI*
C:	HARP BAR • *W. 32nd St., New York, NY*
D:	TWIGS • *Nyack, NY*
E:	*Bristol, RI*

B

B

For newer and more contemporary expressions, the natural wood used to accentuate the relatively open shopfronts is often also used to introduce the interior ambiance. The Mondrian-like arrangement of cubes and rectangles of natural wood in the Napa shop front in Guadalajara also introduces the geometric arrangement of squared off shapes and forms that line the perimeter walls of the long and narrow store.

Similarly, the bold wood constructed entrance into the Planet Earth store makes a striking appearance on the mall aisle and the upswept pylons add even more dynamics to the wood used in the all glass shopfront. Within the store the same wood is used throughout for wall and floor fixtures while reiterating the "nature" in Planet Earth.

The new storefront design for Gymboree combines the new bright pastels with a light, natural wood. The design seems to be constructed of overscaled kiddie building blocks with the simple geometric shapes creating the right look for the children.

The dark stained wood that frames Country Casuals facade reappears as a decorative accent inside the store.

B

B

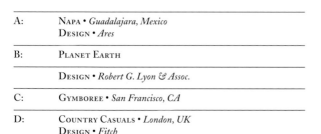

A:	NAPA • *Guadalajara, Mexico*
	DESIGN • *Ares*
B:	PLANET EARTH
	DESIGN • *Robert G. Lyon & Assoc.*
C:	GYMBOREE • *San Francisco, CA*
D:	COUNTRY CASUALS • *London, UK*
	DESIGN • *Fitch*

X-travaganzas

B

Not to be outdone by not having an "X"—these super-scaled, super colossal, spectacular props and storefront treatments add up to X-travaganzas.

Whether it is the new Trojan Horse up in front of FAO Schwarz store bringing gifts to please not only the Greeks but thousands of visitors to the classically-themed Forum in Las Vegas or the giant CocaCola bottle just down Las Vegas Blvd., it is the sheer size that makes these " wonders" overwhelming.

Ron Jon features 30-ft. surfboards while Perfumania is distinguished by the ten-ft. or more perfume bottles that mark out the shop's place in the mall. The over-scaled "bottles" also serve as display windows for the store's products.

Size may not be everything—but it certainly gets attention!

A:	FAO SCHWARZ • *The Forum, Las Vegas NV*
B:	RON JON SURF SHOP DESIGN • *Design Forum*
C/D:	COCACOLA • *Las Vegas Blvd., Las Vegas, NV*
E/F:	PERFUMANIA

A

C

E

F

Yellow

Yellow is springtime. It is daffodils coming up through mounds of snow. It is sunshine: warm and welcoming. It is bright, happy, sunny and funny and it is an in-your-face color. Yellow—from the palest pastel to the richest and deepest earthy ochers "reads" from the distance. It is a color that steps forward to meet you. When buildings are painted yellow or trimmed with yellow they are guaranteed to make a strong statement on the street.

From the examples shown here it would appear that it is a California color since these rehabbed, repainted and redefined shop fronts and buildings are all located on the fun-loving, free-wheeling, and youth oriented streets of Venice and Melrose Ave. in Los Angeles. In subtle contrast is the creamy yellow stucco buildings in Westwood Village in Los Angeles and the ocher gold Starbucks Coffee shop in the lovely old village of Nyack, NY.

A

B

A:	WESTWOOD VOILLAGE • *Los Angeles, CA*
B:	STARBUCKS • *Nyack, NY*
C/D:	MELROSE AVE. • *Los Angeles, CA*
E/F:	MAIN ST. • *Venice, CA*

C

D

E

F

Zig Zag

With the angling of the glass panels in the Honolulu Book store a zig-zag pattern results that also creates a movement towards the entrance of the shop.

The skyscraper in Rosslyn consists of planes moving back and forth—angling in and out—in the set pattern of a saw tooth blade. Here the structures verticality is not emphasized but the strong horizontal bands predominate.

When you zig and zag in horizontal planes the result is a ziggurat-like construction. The multi-stepped roof of the Jewish Museum at the lower tip of Manhattan is an excellent example of that Babylonian temple design revived and updated.

A:	1ST NATIONAL BANK • *Chicago, IL*
B:	SKYSCRAPER • *Rosslyn, VA*
C:	HONOLULU BOOK STORE • *Honolulu, HI* DESIGN • *AM Partners*
D:	JEWISH MUSEUM • *Battery Park, New York, NY*

A

B

"zig zag: a progression characterized by sharp turns first to one side and then the other" creating a saw tooth effect. When planes of a building zig and zag back and forth as they do in the 1st National Bank in Chicago—or in the angled window bays of the building nearby, they create a dramatic vertical play that accentuates the soaring spirit of the design.